VERANDA

A PASSION FOR LIVING

VERANDA

A PASSION FOR LIVING
Houses of Style and Inspiration

CAROLYN ENGLEFIELD

HEARST
books

This book is dedicated in memory of my dear friend, and talented
French photographer *Jacques Dirand*.

HEARSTBOOKS

An Imprint of Sterling Publishing Co., Inc.
1166 Avenue of the Americas
New York, NY 10036

VERANDA is a registered trademark of Hearst Magazine Media, Inc.

ISBN 978-1-61837-135-5

Distributed in Canada by Sterling Publishing Co., Inc.
c/o Canadian Manda Group, 664 Annette Street
Toronto, Ontario M6S 2C8, Canada
Distributed in the United Kingdom by GMC Distribution Services
Castle Place, 166 High Street, Lewes, East Sussex BN7 1XU, England
Distributed in Australia by NewSouth Books
University of New South Wales, Sydney, NSW 2052, Australia

For information about custom editions, special sales, and premium and corporate purchases, please contact
Sterling Special Sales at 800-805-5489 or specialsales@sterlingpublishing.com.

Manufactured in Singapore

6 8 10 9 7 5

sterlingpublishing.com

DESIGNER: Susan Uedelhofen
PHOTO EDITOR: Aleaxandra Brodsky
PUBLISHER: Jacqueline Deval

FOREWORD

Houses are like Wunderkammers to me, those curiosity cabinets of the
Renaissance where each carefully selected object has a story waiting to be told. In fact, oftentimes the cabinets
themselves had equally compelling stories. Small, large, modern minimalism or understudies of grand tour
collecting, our houses mirror ourselves, they tell our story. Like reading a suspense-filled novel where turning
every page reveals a truth, the house we have chosen confirms our convictions, reveals our heart and unlocks
our souls. What could possibly be a more concrete manifestation of self than our home? Ah, yes, maybe the way
we dress each day, but in some ways that is far more ephemeral and fickle than the furnishings and treasures we
have chosen to greet us at the end of a long day, to support our busy daily lives or to share on special occasions
with family and friends.

We are fortunate that each month through the pages of *Veranda* magazine others have chosen to open their
front doors and welcome us into their private worlds. For one house chosen for *Veranda*, many more are reviewed
through the discerning lens called "the Editors Eye." Divining the spirit of the place, feeling the emotions within
and intuiting the story that these houses will reveal has been Carolyn Englefield's joy and passion for as long as
I have known her, my entire career.

Every *Veranda* reader enjoys and relishes those peaceful reading moments while savoring every beautiful
page. I know, having worked with Carolyn on many photo shoots, that she has defined, for me, actually set the
bar for, what I have come to expect in an editor. Directing, producing, feeling a house and revealing its truth,
authenticity and soul is how she would describe her role.

"You just have to believe, be a catalyst, create a dialogue on the page," is how she would describe her brand
of editing. From personal experience I also know that a dose of perfectionism underlies it all. Early morning
hours in flower markets around the world looking for "just the right thing," patiently waiting for the best light,
reviewing the framing of a shot countless times and understanding that the wabi sabi imperfection of a place is
exactly the thing that makes it perfect, are a small part of what this editor's eye brings to each story.

In this volume of European houses Carolyn has once again directed and produced by culling stories of
Veranda's past with the dream of inspiring us now and in the future. *A Passion for Living* is a synthesis of
beliefs as much as it is about style. The belief that our homes are the places where we live our lives with joy,
grace, honesty and personal style. So now, let the stories be told as you turn each page of this Wunderkammer
of European style, sensibility and a soulful outlook on life. —*Charlotte Moss*

PREFACE

Veranda has long had entrée into the world's most beautiful homes and estates—from the Americas to Europe to Asia and beyond. Neither a home's size or cost nor its provenance has ever dictated inclusion in the magazine—places with personality, spunk, character and charm have always overridden houses filled with beige rooms and kitchens that have never been used. That's why a petite Parisian pied-à-terre is as right at home within our pages as a distinguished 18th-century Swedish manoir.

Veranda began as a regional Southern interiors magazine in 1987, yet quickly delved into covering national and international residences, with a special affinity for European houses. While the magazine's name may still hint at a Southern sensibility, certain hallmarks of those initial issues have lived on for almost thirty years: timelessness, graciousness and warmth. Whether a house is in Birmingham, Beverly Hills or Bruges, those three qualities make up a triumvirate of style that defines *Veranda*.

That's also what makes this new book so exciting. In *A Passion for Living*, a compilation of European homes that Carolyn Englefield has produced over the years, the epitome of the *Veranda* lifestyle is evident throughout. And while timelessness is a word and concept that is often overused to the point of cliché, in this book, it's often difficult to pinpoint homes that were designed two, twenty or even two hundred years ago. They are true representatives of good taste and gracious living.

Beyond their homes, Europeans approach life with a certain ease and elegance that Americans often want to emulate. In this far-reaching volume, Carolyn has produced a veritable encyclopedia of European style that anyone can access and find inspiration in—no passport required. —*Clinton Smith, Editor in Chief*

INTRODUCTION

For as long as I can remember, interior visions have always captured my eye. The great privilege—and fun—of being an editor for a magazine like *Veranda* is getting to visit and stay in some of the world's most beautiful homes. In 1994, after working for many years at shelter publications in Manhattan, I moved to Paris as a European correspondent. Fortuitously, I found a quintessential Parisian pied-à-terre while on assignment to shoot Christian Liaigre's home in the magical City of Light, when I asked his then associate India Mahdavi (now a renowned designer in her own right) if I could scout her home for a possible story. When I went to visit her, I fell madly in love with the charming apartment with its small fireplace in the living room and two French doors opening onto a balcony with a view of a church and the rue Moufftard, one of Paris's oldest walking streets with boulangeries, charcuteries and fromageries. I lived at 35 rue Daubenton, in the 5th arrondissement, for thirteen unforgettable, glorious years.

I felt at home in Paris. Everything about living there—the climate, culture, history, food, architecture, landscape—nurtured my soul and creative spirit. I felt a kinship with the European designers, architects, antique dealers, gardeners and photographers whose homes and works are featured in this book. I traveled frequently to Belgium, England, Italy, Sweden and Switzerland as well as all over France in search of residences with an understated elegance and unexpected surprise that would dazzle and inspire magazine readers back home in the United States.

As I started choosing photographs for this book, I knew it must be called A Passion for Living. Europeans have such a natural flair for decorating and creating the perfect backdrop for a meaningful life. Invariably, the homes I like best—the ones that fill me with awe and, yes, a twinge of envy—are owned by passionate collectors whose art and antiques tell the story of their lives. I am drawn to houses with history—the more intriguing the better—which is why I stayed so long in Europe: It was difficult to leave a place where architecture and the decorative arts have flourished for centuries.

During my career, I've developed what I call the Editor's Eye. I can walk into a house and tell almost immediately if it will make a good story. I am always looking for the idiosyncrasies that make a place special. During a photo shoot, which can last for a couple of days, it's my job to intuit the homeowners' intent vision and convey through pictures the spirit of how they live.

I approach photographing a castle or a cottage with equal enthusiasm and discipline. Producing and art-directing photo shoots is more complicated than you'd imagine, but it is the best education in the art of living.

Every situation is different and it is my mission to reveal not just decorating but a way of life. I often buy and arrange the flowers for shoots because people trust me and know I will respect their personal taste. I love to go to the various food markets and purchase local fruits and vegetables that may be used as props and later shared and enjoyed by all (homeowners, designers, photo crew) as a delicious impromptu lunch or dinner.

What makes this book unique is that most of the houses belong to architects, decorators or antiques dealers, so you are seeing their purest style statements, which have not been diluted by the inevitable compromises they must make with clients. I've been an overnight guest in many of these homes, sleeping beneath freshly-pressed linen sheets laced with the scent of local lavender. I've enjoyed alfresco lunches beneath pergolas shaded with wisteria and warmed myself in front of roaring fires on rainy days, chatting about books, movies and the next day's shoot over a glass of wine or a cup of tea. My favorite pastime is frequenting local flea markets in search of hidden treasures to bring home. I appreciate that living well is *la joie de vivre*.

The style secrets I've gleaned from European masters are the raison d'être—the heart and soul—of this book. I have organized the material into four sections so that you can look at the pictures through particular prisms. The first chapter is called "The Art of Imperfection," and you'll see how rooms that don't adhere to convention can be chic and charming. The second chapter on "Personal Style" is a tribute to individuality and how memorable homes reflect their owner's distinct personalities. The third chapter is on "Color," which is the most vital and yet often least understood element in decorating; colors are variable and they take on different moods depending on how and where they are used. The final chapter, "A Sense of Place," makes clear that the best interiors are in dialogue with their exteriors—whether the living room overlooks a Tuscan olive grove or the rooftops of Paris. After all, a happy life means you're in sync with your home and your environment—the seat of your soul.

Every one of the homes on the following pages is special to me. Each has its own magic. They are timeless expressions of what matters most—a passion for living. —*Carolyn Englefield, New York City*

THE ART
OF IMPERFECTION

The magic is in the mix

Creating a home and making it your own is a journey of discovery. Pursued with passion, choosing fabrics, furniture and antiques is a unique, personal reflection of destiny and synchronicity—an aesthetic alchemy of the soul.

Lovingly curated and carefully edited, the houses in this chapter epitomize the poetry of imperfection. Their owners have flawless taste, but their rooms are quirky and unpredictable, while at the same time sophisticated and refined. Eclecticism is the rule, not the exception. The magic is in the mix. And the secret to making magic is following the Laws of Attraction. It's a simple philosophy—and a paradox—that's as old as civilization. You need to understand two tenets: Like Attracts Like and Opposites Attract. To paraphrase F. Scott Fitzgerald, the test of first-rate decorating is the ability to hold two opposing ideas in the mind at the same time.

With its mix of stone floors, galvanized buckets, copper pots and roaming hens, the potting shed at Belgian *antiquaire* Jean-Philippe Demeyer's 17th-century Medieval manor outside Bruges is wonky and wonderful; visually compelling but utilitarian, too.

"The most important thing is not the furniture. It is the atmosphere." —*Jean-Philippe Demeyer*

OPPOSITE Jean-Philippe Demeyer walking with his black retrievers on the drive bordered by a tree-lined allée at his home outside of Bruges. ABOVE Unexpected and unconventional, the bold *pointe de diamant* pattern painted on the 17th-century walls looks modern but is actually adapted from a historic Belgian design. By contrasting antique Gothic chairs and an elegant linen tablecloth with rustic stone floors, Demeyer created a dining room with a unique personality that is painterly, playful and melodic.

21

Instead of being in thrall to history, Demeyer created a library with an amusing, contemporary vibe. Each piece of furniture has its own personality, responding to and engaging with the others. Strong, vivid colors create an uplifting energy that's both irreverent and respectful of the past.

Juxtaposing the formal with the informal, the modern with the antique, the precious with the commonplace, houses develop their own personality and character. The layering of diverse furniture, fabrics and objets d'art is especially appealing when they all have a patina. Whether faded, nicked, cracked or mellowed and ripened by age, furnishings that evince a tangible sense of their past offer profound grace notes in any interior. When periods and provenances are judiciously mixed, rooms become evocative reflections of their inhabitants that inspire me, filling my mind with ideas and my heart with joy. They are labors of love that prove that living well *is* the best revenge.

Designed by the Belgian antiques dealer Axel Vervoordt, who is one of the most inspiring, enlightening, soulful, talented and intelligent men I know, the stair hall in this renovated castle is hung with Old Master drawings, *trompe l'oeil* and grisaille paintings. Nothing is treated as precious, but everything demands your attention and piques your curiosity.

OPPOSITE Axel Vervoordt is known for interiors that are uncontrived and unforced, such as this foyer, which has the spirit of a Renaissance *cabinet de curiosités*. The graphic quality of the floor, the softness of the draped linen table topped by books and objets d'art makes it a place you want to linger at. ABOVE The warmth of aged ceiling beams in the dining room is a striking contrast to walls the color of terra-cotta mixed with redbrick dust. Surrounded by simple linen-covered chairs, the bare wood table is set with antique pewter plates, silver and glass that evoke the mood of a Flemish painting.

"I juxtapose major pieces with more everyday objects to retain a human dimension."

—*Axel Vervoordt*

Designed by Jacques, Martin and Peter Wirtz, the garden's magic comes from mixing English and Italian landscape traditions, creating a labyrinth that draws you in.

Eclectic decorating is becoming de rigueur in the United States, but it's a style we've adapted from the Europeans.

More than a "look," it's an attitude that's second nature in countries with long histories. The Italians have centuries of art and architecture to inspire them, and they are masters of the mix. They intuitively know how to combine elements—humble, tribal or regional items with finer things like a hand blown Murano glass chandelier and Wedgwood china—that are unexpectedly but absolutely complementary. Rooms that are relaxed yet pulled-together, breathtaking yet welcoming, always make me feel at home. The ultimate luxury is knowing who you are and how you want to live.

In the dining room of their house in the countryside near Como, Nicola and Elda Fabrizio—the founders of DEDAR (DEsign D'ARredamento—Design for Interiors)—used one of their regional fabrics for the curtains to frame the view to the garden. By setting the linen-draped table surrounded by wicker chairs with rustic placemats and fine china and crystal, they created a space that feels right for both family meals and formal entertaining.

One of the hallmarks of Italian country style is to upholster important antiques, like this Biedermeier sofa, with plain linen. Other fabrics play off the colors in the large painting of a ruin by Luca Pignatelli. Modern lamps and a side table crammed with books contribute to the contemporary mood imbued with genuine Old World charm.

ABOVE A 19th-century French painting hangs over a Chinese table with a curious display of sculptural objects that invite contemplation. OPPOSITE A guest bedroom is a marvelous mélange. Century-old beams contrast with a contemporary cast-iron canopy bed by Paola Navone for Cappellini and the classic modern reading lamp by Artemide. The photograph leaning against the wall on the floor next to the DEDAR curtains of Coco Chanel sums up the owner's insouciant style.

There is always a rhyme or reason to the way a stylish home is decorated, but it is not necessarily obvious.

The combination of good taste and gut instincts is highly individual, and the lesson is to follow your own inner voice and creative compass. Architect Piero Castellini Baldissera's apartment in the 15th-century Casa degli Atellani reflects the broad interests of the designer of fabrics for Milan's C&C. Like all mix-maestros, he is expert at layering textures and objects, and walking through his home offers climax after climax—an explosive visual experience. Luxurious without being formidable, his home invites discovery, conversation and inspiration.

Old-world formality has never been so friendly as in Piero Castellini Baldissera's 15th-century apartment in Milan. OPPOSITE TOP LEFT The breathtaking domed ballroom, which has 17th-century frescoes, is where he hosts concerts and family reunions. TOP RIGHT In the dining room, a tin chandelier with real candles from a Ligurian church hangs above a beautifully polished Louis XV table. BOTTOM The slip-covered chairs seem to be dancing across the bare wood floors. The saffron-striped curtains have a warm glow, filtering and enhancing the sunlight.

The foyer has been designed as an enchanting winter garden with trompe l'oeil walls of potted plants. Instead of treating the magnificent Directoire settee from Napoleon's sister's house in Parma as a museum piece, Castellini used it to create a tableau with books and pictures. Behind it, the Louis XVI screen topped by gilded arrowheads, which used to be covered in fabric, becomes a piece of sculpture. The leather rhino that seems to be crisscrossing the room adds to the surreal atmosphere.

Entering the living room from the winter garden is like walking into a new painting. It's upright, not uptight, rich and lavish without being fussy. The informally constructed, unlined curtains don't take themselves too seriously, setting a tone where anyone could feel at home.

The master bedroom is a cultivated, aristocratic balance of the feminine and masculine—Napoleon and Josephine, yin and yang. All of the golden striped fabrics are from C&C and complement the striped walls. Collections of intaglios, obelisks, photographs and paintings make the room personal and meaningful.

Remember the magic is

comes from what you expe

expect. It's the unexpecte

unconventional touches th

room, giving its unique cha

in the mix…and rarely

ct—but from what you don't

d, whimsical surprises and

at make a difference in a

acter and personal charm.

ABOVE At their historic Flemish estate, Belgian designers Alain and Brigitte Garnier designed an entrance hall with a sculptural cement-and-oak staircase. Old world and modern at the same time, it is finished in gray-brown chalk plaster that is warm, earthy and rich. OPPOSITE The spectacular Italian family Tree of Life painting is paired with an antique bench upholstered in Belgian silk with throw pillows casually arranged in an irreverent fashion.

The chic dining room is multidimensional with undeniable flair. The use of oversized pieces creates drama and proves that any great room is based on scale—bigger is almost always better! The low-hung chandelier creates a sense of intimacy paired with a table topped by two cloths—crisp, scalloped linen over an elaborately embroidered one. A wall-length French cupboard has an enviable presence that provides character as well as display space for a lovely collection of celadon porcelain and antique coffee pots.

A former pig barn was turned into a vaulted kitchen with a thatched roof. On the stone terrace, a simple raw wood table is set for Sunday lunch with antique blue-and-white china, a compelling high/low mix that is elegant, welcoming and unpretentious.

The Art of Imperfection requires defying convention and trusting your instincts. Creative expression in making a home must be a personal statement even when you are working with an architect or decorator. The house on the following pages in the south of France has an idiosyncratic charm that reflects the sensibility of the owner, who is nearly blind. Nonetheless, her aesthetic sense is so pronounced that it gives form to feelings.

During the thirteen years I lived in Paris, I came to appreciate how Europeans think of their homes as works in progress, continually layering in new acquisitions that keep their residences from feeling like museums. The juxtaposition of elements—old and new, urbane and rustic, shimmer and matte—makes a house relevant, dynamic and alive.

Restored by architect Gilles Gregoire, the formerly abandoned three-hundred-year-old Provençal farmhouse has a soulful stylishness. The Louis XV stone fireplace was found at a salvage dealer near Lyon. The antique Italian fauteuils are upholstered in vintage damask that make them feel like treasured family heirlooms. The Italian doorframe is incongruous yet harmonious.

The serene grand salon demonstrates the poetry of patina. An Aubusson tapestry is casually draped over a Provençal sofa, with antique lanterns providing illumination. The centerpiece of the room is an oversized Swedish painted table surrounded by Italian chairs with linen slipcovers. Empty gilt-wood frames and a shelf holding candlesticks create an arresting tableau on the muted gray walls.

ABOVE The interior architecture is slightly modern, which is a wonderful contrast to the diverse assortment of antiques. The furniture arrangement is flexible, allowing the room to be used night and day for intimate tête-à-têtes or large parties, a place of contemplation or conversation. The combination of elements makes the room serene yet spirited.

r friends.

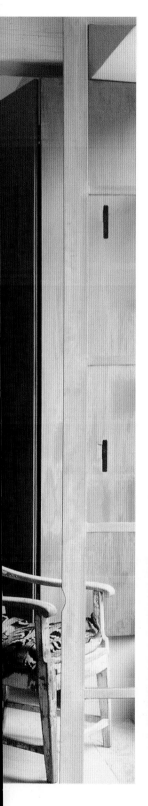

ABOVE A coronet of crunchy, textured fabric over the daybed piled with soft pillows makes the guest room a coveted refuge. A cabinet of curiosities contains apothecary jars and *herbiers*. The homeowner's generosity of spirit is evident in the way she shares her passions with her guests.

A passion for living is often revealed in the simplest details.

Fresh flowers bring any room to life. A few peonies from the garden are a personal touch that resonates when placed in a simple glass vase on an antique table with a luscious patina.

Collect what you love. One of the most important lessons I ever learned was to shop with an open heart and mind. By all means, carry a tape measure with you wherever go, so you don't buy an armoire that won't fit through the front door. If you follow your instincts and stay true to your own taste, the art, objects and furniture you collect will naturally work together. There is no wrong direction as long as it is right for you.

Go to museums and historic houses to develop what I call the Editor's Eye, the ability to go to a flea market or secondhand store and zoom in on the diamonds in the rough, the things that make your heart race. The world is full of beautiful, remarkable things and living with some of them offers comfort and joy.

For a bachelor pad in Paris, decorator Bruno de Caumont started with the owner's collection of 19th-century antiques and flea-market finds. The jaunty lilac-and-cream striped walls in the main salon are an original and surprisingly sympathetic backdrop for a diverse art collection.

Tailored and theatrical, the dining room doubles as a library, a stimulating backdrop for dinner parties or quiet meditation. Pale lavender walls and a poppy-colored cloth are a nice counterpoint to the Napoleonic iron chandelier and classical statue in the alcove.

"Color can reveal so much about someone's personality. But people don't want to reveal the truth about who they are."

—*Bruno de Caumont*

The use of lilac as a leitmotif creates a sense of harmony in rooms full of diverse objects. The dramatic col carré silk lantern by Thomas Boog is an idiosyncratic gesture that adds a modern touch to an old-world room that includes Chinese scrolls and Empire and Louis XIII–style furniture, along with drawings by Christian Berard and Pierre Le-Tan.

A 17th-century cabinet was turned into a cabinet of curiosities, which is an appropriate metaphor for an entire apartment that abounds in fascinating details and collections that don't necessarily have provenance but nonetheless reveal the owner's particular tastes and personal style.

The bones of an old house are always worth preserving. When designer Frédéric Méchiche bought a humble three-hundred-year-old house in coastal Provence, he was determined to honor its history and the passage of time. He sanded down the plaster walls to highlight their imperfection and rusticity, revealing layers of color from pale blue to gray, which have the texture of a painter's canvas. If only these walls could talk!

Saving an old house does not mean you need to try to recreate a bygone era or turn it into a diorama. You can refurbish it with care and furnish it with pieces that would have never belonged to the previous inhabitants. You can mash-up sensibilities and styles as long as your point of view is consistent and your choices are well-considered.

The 18th-century plank-top table with treillage apron might have been originally made in Paris for a country house. The 18th-century silver, glassware and china are fancier than the rustic surroundings, but the table setting is modern and appropriate. The circa 1820s bird centerpiece is from the Capodimonte factory in Naples.

The silhouettes of the antique furniture are highlighted by simple upholstery fabrics such as plain muslin or linen. The nail heads are often left exposed, a modern "deconstructed" approach to using antiques. The small scale of the crystal chandelier is surprising and provocative, emphasizing its contrarian preciousness in this rather raw yet simply elegant space.

OPPOSITE A weathered cabinet is the perfect complement to a collection of mystical, otherworldly objects that seem like treasures rescued from a sunken ship. BELOW A mix of antique indigo striped fabrics illustrates how simplicity and irreverence can be sublime bedfellows. The casually draped valance adds to the romance of sleeping under luxurious linen sheets and reading by candlelight.

"The welcoming, spicy scent of age-old wood greeted me."

—*Charles Spada*

Boston designer Charles Spada bought his 1652 brick-and-stone house in Normandy because of its intrinsic charm and intact architecture, so when he realized the best place for the leopard-silk canapé to go was in front of the original billiards cabinet he merely shut the doors instead of making alterations. He kept the original painted finish on the boiserie after washing it down with lye. A mammoth Swedish chandelier is a dazzling counterpoint to the weathered 17th-century floors.

Spada converted the library into the master suite, placing the upholstered headboard up against the existing bookshelves. His restrained use of a woodsy botanical fabric shows how floral patterns can be unexpectedly masculine. My Editor's Eye was struck by the vignette across from the bed: the combination of empty Louis XIII frames, antique drawings, iron sconces and a lovely creamware tureen is the signature of a passionate collector.

As the American designer Steven Shubel proves in his Paris pied-à-terre, you can live dramatically and comfortably in a small space. Located in a 17th-century building in the Marais, the one-room studio is reached by a steep staircase that creates a sense of anticipation that is more than met as you enter this jewel-box apartment.

Every square inch delights the senses, which all good decorating should do. His supreme accomplishment is having created a space that is grand and intimate, personal and inviting, whimsical and functional. Of course, it helps that the apartment was on the *piano nobile* with high beamed ceilings and tall windows, but it's especially enchanting because of its subtle eccentricity.

An oversized gilt-wood mirror is dramatic and expansive, reflecting the romantic view of Parisian courtyard. An 18th-century plaster frieze hangs next to it.

A room for all reasons, Shubel sleeps, dines and entertains easily in his pied-à-terre, where a pair of mattresses doubles as a daybed. His diverse assortment of objects and artworks all work together because they are united by his singular sensibility.

ABOVE The dogs feel quite at home on the chairs surrounding a 19th-century table placed in front of the window. OPPOSITE Dressed with a coverlet from Liwan and a silk pillow, the banquette becomes the bed in the evenings where Shubel can read or dream about the City of Light.

PERSONAL
STYLE

*Knowing who you are
and how you want to live*

Our homes should reflect the purest expression of our hopes, dreams and individuality. The combination of creativity, intuition, confidence and fearlessness is how we manifest our passion for living well.

Homes with great style are not only about what you see but also about what you *feel*. They are captivating—places you never want to leave. The personalities of people with great taste and a strong sense of themselves are reflected in the way they live and decorate.

The houses and apartments in this chapter have been designed with intention, rigor and discipline. Whether their owners are traditionalists, modernists or minimalists, their point of view is well-defined and refined, distinctive and unique. Veere Grenney and David Oliver's grand apartment on the banks of the River Thames in London, which dates to 1879, is a beautiful confluence of sensibilities, a home that tells you the story of their lives.

An alumnus of the venerable English decorating firm Colefax and Fowler, designer Veere Grenney marries a traditionalist's reverence for scale, suitability and proportion with modern art and furniture. Collaborating with his partner, David Oliver, the design director of the Paint & Paper Library, they combined classical architectural moldings with a sleek mantel and a glamorous Jansen chandelier with artworks by Alexander Calder. Their timeless dining room is the epitome of urban chic.

In the living room, Grenney and Oliver trusted their well-honed intuition, defying convention by opting for a monochromatic palette—not the norm for London homes, which typically rely on color to compensate for the city's preponderance of gray days. The mantel, mirror and furniture are all custom; they were designed to make the room as bright and comfortable as possible.

The bedroom pays homage to classic Colefax and Fowler style in a clean, contemporary way. The exquisite bed hangings are a nod to England's tradition of fine tailoring. The nuanced gray color palette was inspired by the light and atmosphere of London, and the gilt-framed artworks add just the right touch of sparkle to the room.

"Everything I do is very considered but still looks casual. Supreme elegance starts with comfort: the most important thing in the world."

—*Veere Grenney*

David Hicks, the legendary English decorator, was a man of few words. His London pied-à-terre is an eloquent testament to his rebellious spirit that was tempered by a reverence for tradition. His ability to work within classic idioms and make them seem fresh endeared him to his clients and stylish people around the globe. He had a great sense of scale and proportion, and he would always inject modern touches—like his much-imitated geometric fabrics and rugs—that were just right for the go-go 1960s and still look correct today.

Confident and audacious, he was well aware of his role as an arbiter of style. "My greatest contribution as an interior designer has been to show people how to use bold color mixtures, and how to mix old with new."

David Hicks's cultivated sensibility is expressed in the way he arranged fine objects—English pottery urns, a South African stone head, an 18th-century lead bust of Mercury—on an 1830s William Kent eagle table with a top of scrubbed Hornton stone.

With walls painted the color of Coca-Cola, Hicks's living room has a strict symmetry that reflects his controlled approach and dramatic nature. Its formality is mitigated by one of his trademark geometric rugs and the simple unlined silk taffeta curtains that allow daylight to filter in.

The daybed Hicks designed for himself has a severe, monastic beauty. Its modern lines are contrasted with gilt swan chairs in the Directoire style that are treated more like sculpture than furniture. The plaster frieze above the bed is a copy of one in the Parthenon.

Wonderful homes have a sense of place. They are informed by their history and location as much as by their architecture. Susan Gutfreund's Paris apartment in a *hôtel particulier* in the chic Faubourg Saint-Germain (where her next-door neighbor is haute couturier Hubert de Givenchy) is an American's expression of a passion for French culture and the traditions of the 7th Arrondissement.

The grand residence also reflects her role as one of the world's most generous and inspirational hostesses, who treats all her guests like visiting royalty. Working side-by-side with the master French decorator Henri Samuel, Gutfreund created a home that is ultra-elegant and surprisingly warm—a testament to her cultivated taste and savoir faire.

A grand staircase sets the tone as guests ascend to Susan Gutfreund's pied-à-terre on the piano nobile in a *hôtel particulier* on the Left Bank in Paris.

The grand salon is a paean to understated elegance and restraint. The ethereal, monochromatic palette is the ideal backdrop for parties where the guests are often dressed in the latest Paris fashions. Pale, striped-cotton summer slipcovers create a casual mood in a setting with elaborate boiserie and fine antiques—the decorating white-on-white equivalent of wearing a Gap T-shirt with a Chanel suit.

The dining room's walls feature eight antique French panels of the muses. Surrounded by silk-upholstered chairs beneath a Russian chandelier, the table is rarely set the same way twice. Dining at the Gutfreunds is always a memorable experience for both the food (she is always to willing to share a recipe) and the tablescapes (such as a centerpiece of roses and fresh mint).

al." *—Susan Gutfreund*

The master suite is a cocoon of Braquenié fabric. It's unabashedly feminine, which is fitting because Gutfreund is a lady's lady: She attends personally to all the finishing touches that make a house a home. Her rooms always have fresh flowers and scented candles burning. She credits her decorator with teaching her the art of living. "Working with Henri was a master class," she says.

A beautiful home speaks for itself. French decorator Jean-Loup Daraux's home in the Camargue countryside in the south of France tells you everything you need to know about his belief in the *douceur de vivre*—the sweet life.

You know from the moment you enter the front hall that you've arrived at a seductive country estate that was designed for leisure and recreation. The antlers that line the staircase hint at hunting parties and the urn with walking sticks suggests afternoon rambles in the woods. "What is essential is to speak to the imagination," he says. "When you speak to the imagination, absolutely everyone understands."

The entry has a noble quality, as if you'd happened upon a castle in rural Ireland. It's grand but informal, with chairs to make it easy to change out of your boots after a walk. The iron stair rail is original to the house, which was rebuilt in the neo-Romantic, post-Revolutionary fashion by a princely Italian family.

The living room's trompe l'oeil paneling and Delftville fireplace surround are a vivid foil for gilt Italian sconces, antique Chinese vases and Louis XIV armchairs, creating the mood of a Mad Hatter's tea party. It is a personal fantasy that seems to exist in another time or place while feeling exactly right for Daraux, who's a passionate collector of antiques and objets d'art.

"The dining room is the most important room in the house."

—Jean-Loup Daraux

With its trompe l'oeil walls, the dining room feels like a three-dimensional painting. Venetian 18th-century chairs surround a wood tabletop set on Roman stone pedestals. It's an ideal environment for Daraux to set the table imaginatively with his extensive and eclectic collection of dishes and glasses.

BELOW In the "bird bedroom," engravings by George Buffon are hung in trompe l'oeil frames. OPPOSITE In the master suite, trompe l'oeil medallions add a romantic flavor as do the upholstered headboards in a checkerboard fabric.

"I like organized disor

flowers everywhere, fir

laid tables that bring

emotion—a magical

douceur de vivre, the

der, natural materials,

eplaces and beautifully

warmth, intimacy and

atmosphere of French

sweet life." —Jean-Loup Daraux

Personal style is not always about putting your own stamp on a home; sometimes, it's about leaving well enough alone, respecting and honoring history. ABOVE The painted doors and doorframe are quirky and inviting. OPPOSITE The well-worn stone steps evoke centuries of use by previous occupants of Jean-Loup Daraux's house, but the trompe l'oeil walls are his signature touch—they look as if they might have always been there.

113

The guest room demonstrates the glories of idiosyncrasy. Both the Venetian mirror and 18th-century desk have their original, well-earned patina. They are set against a faded blue, lime-washed wall. The 18th-century wrought-iron bed frame is from an Italian convent and the antique quilts are from Provence.

Personal style does not have to be heavy-handed. Dick Vervoordt, who grew up in a 14th century Belgian castle, now lives in a rustic 1945 farmhouse in a village outside of Antwerp that is very different than his childhood home. It shares many aesthetic qualities with his parents' more elaborate residence: purity, eclecticism, timelessness, subdued coloring and an inspired use of old materials.

"Our idea was to keep the house simple and contemporary but with a warm feeling," says Vervoordt. While all the windows are new, the exterior brick walls are original and the interior walls are white or brown, and some were colored with earth from the property. Modest for a house that is 7,200 square feet, it is sophisticated yet practical for a young family.

Pine tree trunks with a sculptural quality support the roof of the veranda, where the family gathers for Sunday luncheons. The deft mix of wood, wicker and brick is both austere and warm, painstakingly considered but not the least bit fussy.

The living room is minimal and modern, cozy and drop-dead chic. Traditional armchairs with washed, faded linen slipcovers are meant for relaxation. The room is tranquil without being boring, uncluttered yet rich with character.

The dining room doubles as a library, and it was decorated to create a mood that does not limn any specific period or style. Every object possesses its own character. The thoughtful integration of furnishings establishes an ambience where life can be lived to its fullest.

Every moment, Isabelle de Borchgrave lives her life as an artist, which is evident in every square inch of her 1904 townhouse in Brussels. Every breath she takes is an expression of her creativity as a painter, costume designer and decorator. The house is a series of vignettes and compositions pulled together by her singular vision and artistic hand.

Christian Liaigre's weekend home in Île de Ré, France, is the apotheosis of his modernist aesthetic. The rigor of his minimalist point of view pays homage to the traditions of the fishermen who've long called this island home. "There is a not a grain of excess in the way people here have always lived," he says.

Eclecticism is at its most elegant in de Borchgrave's library/game room, which is located between the living and dining rooms. The small scale of the rug in front of the fireplace is deliberate. "I love carpets that aren't the size of the room," she says. "They're like paintings on the floor."

"I want art
to be
the totality
of my life.
Memories,
thoughts,
and ideas—
there are
so many
things in
our heads."

—*Isabelle de Borchgrave*

The layering of textiles that capture her imagination gives the living room its warmth and soul. The chandelier is made of crystals she collected. The wall hanging is a framed 17th-century Italian textile that she found at the flea market in Provence.

BELOW The table is set with a plate that de Borchgrave designed for her line of faience for Gien. She also designs Beauville tablecloths, Caspari stationery and Villeroy & Boch tiles. OPPOSITE The dining room has the feeling of an artist's atelier with the natural light streaming in. It's a riot of randomness—chalky white chairs, a scrubbed wood table, blue-and-white ginger jars, Portuguese porcelain, Chinese verre églomisé portraits, her own abstract painting—that is nevertheless harmonious.

De Borchgrave's *papiers à la mode*—exquisite paper dresses evoking high fashions from the courts of the Medici in the Renaissance to the legendary Fortuny silks of the early 20th century—are displayed in the house. They caused a sensation in France when they were first shown and are the subject of the book *Paper Illusions: The Art of Isabelle de Borchgrave.*

In her colorful and whimsical bedroom, de Borchgrave plays sure-handedly with pattern. Instead of a chaise longue in the sitting room, she has a work table where she can paint, draw and write. She hand-painted the valance and the borders of the curtains made from Jim Thompson cotton-silk fabric.

Furniture designer Christian Liaigre—who was as responsible as anyone for the high-glamour modernist revival of the 1990s—has an intentionally modest weekend home in Île de Ré, France, which honors the traditional island lifestyle. "In the old days, sailors returned home from voyages with furniture in the dark woods I love," he says. "I wanted my house to make reference to both their travels and my own. Everything I put in it is like a souvenir brought back from an exotic trip."

The only element in the eat-in kitchen that Liaigre did not design himself is the fireplace. The pine cupboards are topped with a teak counter he stained with tar "because it amused me to use the same product Île de Ré sailors use on their boat hulls." The chestnut stools were inspired by Adirondack furniture. The table, bench and picture rail with framed navigation maps are all made of African wenge wood.

"I am always digging for the roots that reveal a place."

—Christian Liaigre

The four-poster bed that Liaigre designed in wenge wood for the master bedroom was inspired by the Shakers. He is proud that the house does not have central heating. "This is a vacation house," he says. "In winter, we get along just fine with heavy sweaters and lighting a fire."

Jacques Grange is one of France's most acclaimed and recognized designers. His work is never formulaic and he does not have a signature "look." Every project has a freshness, as if you're seeing something you'd never seen before.

His farmhouse in Provence is the purest expression of his style philosophy because it has not been filtered through the needs of a client. There is an effortlessness to the way it has been decorated. It is the quintessence of the European sensibility where entertaining at home is an essential ritual. The art of living depends on sharing your home with friends and family. After the furniture has been arranged, the curtains and artwork hung, a house is not finished; it is only the beginning....

The back of the ivy-draped L-shaped house is a romantic locale for casual entertaining. The unstudied beauty of the garden seems to guarantee that guests will be comfortable and that the conversation will be lively and convivial.

In the living room, Grange—who is by turns funny and serious, flamboyant and self-effacing—left the wall behind the Jean-Michel Frank sofa empty to create a serene mood. The furniture is arranged to facilitate engaging conversation.

stablished taste." *—Jacques Grange*

With its stuffed animals and wooden zebra, the bedroom reflects Grange's whimsical side. Mosquito netting is draped over a bed made with luxurious linen sheets. The mise-en-scène is undeniably original, like the designer himself.

COLOR

The backdrop of our lives

Is there any decision more personal than our choice of colors? It's a reflection of our spirit, as crucial as whom we love and just as vital to our happiness. It is not a question of just what we see—but rather how it makes us feel.

There is nothing more powerful than color. It affects every aspect of our lives, influencing our moods, thoughts and spiritual energy. Everyone has an emotional component, and the primary colors, of course, are foundational. **Red,** the color of love, connotes warmth, courage, strength, excitement; it is passionate and stimulating. Blue represents intelligence, signifying trust, serenity and logic; it is essentially soothing. Yellow signifies emotional strength, representing creativity, confidence, optimism; the right yellow elevates our spirits and our self-esteem. While the meanings of colors depend on cultural context and can change over time, their ability to affect our moods is a constant.

At Château de Montigny, London designer Andrew Allfree's 18th-century, Louis XIII–style home in Normandy, strong colors give a classical house a contemporary vibe. The contrast of hot-pink Indian fabric and snow-white boiserie is a bold backdrop for a blue Murano chandelier, a Genoese white marble console, a Roman granite vase, an English oak chair, a Victorian spoon-back easy chair and a Mogul rug.

BELOW Tractor-green woodwork and earthy walls—a combination borrowed from the surrounding farm fields—unites disparate elements in the study, where a pair of antique white marble urns sit in the window. Antique leather-bound books were chosen specifically for the color of their spines. OPPOSITE The summer bedroom is painted the color of the sky on a clear day in July; a persimmon velvet curtain is casually draped over an early-19th-century Regency sofa.

ABOVE Green, the color of balance, provides equilibrium even when used with verve and zest in the main salon of Château de Montigny. The gilt-wood overdoors are original. A pair of Louis XV Revival chairs complement the banquette upholstered in an antique silver-and-blue damask. OPPOSITE The midnight-blue walls give the bedroom a sense of tranquillity despite the over-the-top George III gilded bed covered in 18th-century damask and lined with emerald-green silk from India. A pair of English Greek Revival satinwood sidechairs at the foot of the bed sit on a sapphire-blue Agra rug.

"There is no blue without yellow a

nd without orange."—*Vincent van Gogh*

Lars Sjöberg has restored his estate in Uppland, Sweden, to recapture the aura of the 18th century. ABOVE An 18th-century flip-top table with its original paint holds an antique Chinese bowl filled with clementines that provide a refreshing jolt of energetic color. OPPOSITE A Gustavian bed is draped with indigo-and-white fabric by Ljungbergs after antique linen.

Trust your intuition when choosing colors, but don't make decisions based on whim. The light and landscape are crucial. At his farmhouse in Tuscany, Piero Castellini Baldissera, one of Italy's most revered interior architects and cofounder of C&C Milano, was inspired by nature—fields of lavender, local raspberries and lush peonies. The palette he chose is sensuous and vibrant. The colors are intense, but so is the man himself; he has well-honed instincts. "The architecture is so nice by itself that it's very difficult to do anything better," he says. But he could never live without color. "I would say my style is a non-style. I put things together in ways that you're not supposed to and in the end, I find something perfect for me."

In the dining room of his farmhouse, Piero Castellini Baldissera, inspired by a trip to North Africa, designed chairs that he upholstered in delicious sorbet-colored linen. The walls throughout the house are hand-painted in the many hues of Tuscan sunsets.

It's always a sunny day inside Castellini's farmhouse, and bowls of fresh fruit and vases filled with fresh flowers complement the color palette of his home. Traditional furniture such as English Colonial-style chairs are upholstered in contemporary C&C fabrics.

"Tuscan colors are magnetic."

ABOVE Inspired by gardens where flowers of different shades always seem to harmonize, Castellini is a mix-maestro who combines strong colors with an effortlessness informed by a disciplined eye. In a guest room, the flower arrangement reflects his bold yet nuanced approach.

—*Piero Castellini Baldissera*

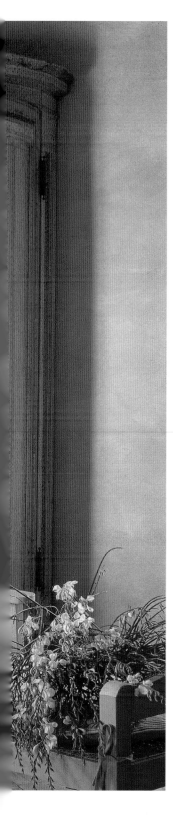

ABOVE In another guest room, pale lilac linens and fabrics are paired with moss-green walls in a sophisticated and soothing manner. Violet, the color of spirituality, encourages contemplation while also feeling luxurious because it's a color associated with refinement, quality and royalty.

Everything has a color, so all the elements inside or outside a house are critical to the composition. For a client who had bought the rundown 18th-century Château du Tertre in the Margaux wine country northwest of Bordeaux, the Belgian designer Axel Vervoordt was as concerned with the exterior as the interior when he oversaw its renovation and decoration. Built of pale yellow stone, the house is framed by verdant green lawns, a bank of trees, a stately orangerie and a reflecting pool that masquerades as an ornamental *bassin*. The pastel-colored landscape is a fitting prelude to the interiors, which feature rooms painted sky blue or the golden hues of the late afternoon sun. The secret of color is the atmosphere it creates.

Axel Vervoordt approached Château de Tertre as an artist would with respect to the landscape (designed by Jacques Wirtz) that is as well composed as any en plein air painting.

Walls painted the color of wheat are an exquisite backdrop for glamorous, gilt Baroque benches. The center table's iridescent, silk moiré blue skirt floats in the middle of the entrance hall as if it were a pool of water. A mix of Gustavian and French chairs give the space a classic, timeless quality.

The living room's sky-blue walls are painted in a manner that has depth and dimension, so you feel as if you are floating in mid air. And yet the room is very grounded with comfortable club chairs slipcovered in plain linen. The lack of pattern is intentional. "My way of working is almost no décor," says Vervoordt. "It's about restoring an architecture to make it look as good as possible with the right floors, beautiful panels and old doors. Then, put great things in it, and choose the right discreet colors."

Depending on its application, color can be architecture's friend or foe. In his pied-à-terre in the Marais near the Place des Vosges, the Argentine designer Roberto Bergero counter-intuitively used strong hues to accentuate his apartment's exquisite moldings and woodwork which are painted in pristine white. "I treat interiors as if they were stage sets," he says. When he found his apartment, the walls were a chic but understated Versailles gray, and he painted them a vivid Tyrrhenian pink. He designed the apple-green screen in front of the fireplace as well as the hand-painted rug.

His bold approach is not for the faint of heart; he considers taking risks one of the perquisites of his profession. "It's a decorator's privilege," he says.

The living room's mise-en-scène is carefully and artfully composed. Instead of compromising the architecture, the hot-pink walls ennoble the apartment's 19th-century bones.

ABOVE The dining room is a play of vivid contrasts with a white-painted Louis XV–style bergère juxtaposed with color-saturated walls, a crystal chandelier and a custom wood-and-gesso screen. CENTER An antique Sevres porcelain figure and an Italian ex-voto are one of the many grace notes throughout Bergero's apartment.

ABOVE Bergero sure-handedly mixes eras and motifs, using a variety of art, objects and textiles to create a colorful medley. The bedspread is made from antique Swedish fabric. The custom headboard is a hand-painted canvas.

The secret language of color: P

love, nurturing and sexuality.

it can evoke glamour and sc

everything. WHITE, the antit

and reflection of pure light. W

and clarity. It makes all colors

INK is the color of femininity,

BLACK is all colors absorbed;

phistication, a complement to

nesis of black; a manifestation

hite promises simplicity, purity

n the rainbow inevitable.

We all know that a quick coat of paint is the surest way to transform a space. At their 17th-century estate in the Berry region of central France, interior designer Michelle Halard and her husband, Yves, are forever remaking and recoloring their rooms. She explains that her home is in a constant state of flux and metamorphosis because of her restless creativity and desire for her surroundings to always seem fresh and alive. "I cannot think of anything more tiresome in the realm of decoration than visiting a house and seeing something as incidental as a carafe posed in a certain way in a certain place—and returning twenty years later and seeing that it hasn't budged." It's that *je ne sais quoi* that makes their home so inviting, intriguing and compelling. "A room is the suit of the soul," is a favorite quote of hers by Jean Cocteau.

The walls are painted a soulful saffron in the music room, which occupies one of the château's two towers. Michelle says she "rescued" fifty-year-old flea market gilt chairs by upholstering them in shocking-pink cotton for an effect that is modern and whimsical.

Bolts of Aurelie fabric are used lavishly in a bedroom to create a blue cocoon that with one grand, signature gesture is regal, crisp, stunning and forever chic.

"With a
few meters
of cotton,
I can do more
to change
the atmosphere
of a room
than with an
entire suite
of furniture."

—*Michelle Halard*

There is no fabric more quintessentially French than toile de Jouy, and the Halards created a big splash in a the bathroom by using the famous La Dame du Lac print lavishly on the walls, windows and furniture

Throughout Europe, some of the most beautiful houses and châteaux are made of stone in every imaginable shade of gray. Although stately and regal, these architectural marvels often lack a joie de vivre, which helps explain why the careful use of cheerful colors is essential to the European approach to decorating.

Improvisation is not a word that interior designers often use. They find a rug or painting and then set about decorating a room very deliberately with complementary colors. But French couturier Michel Klein and his longtime associate Joel Fournier, who are control freaks when it comes to making clothes, let their impulses and imaginations guide them when they decorated their 1595 Provençal farmhouse. Instead of planning, they created colors on the spot, mixing acrylic paint with natural pigment thinned with water so the old walls looked washed with dynamic colors—from roasted orange and royal purple to ocherous yellow and aqueous blue—which infused their rooms with spirited style. It's important to remember color can enhance, embellish and adorn a room, so don't be afraid to make a bold statement.

Although it's a country house, the owners consider their living room "very Parisian." An eye-popping Régence-style Napoleon III mirror hangs over an oak buffet. The signed Louis XV armchair is upholstered in a jaunty stripe.

BELOW A whimsically painted door adds verve to a small guest room. The bed's tester is wrapped with an Indian sari and Balinese batiks. The parakeet-feather headdress comes from the South Seas. OPPOSITE Several shades of blue harmonize in a children's guest room with twin wrought-iron beds designed by Fournier. The unlined curtains are intentionally casual but the gilt valance is raffiné.

"Love is a canvas furnished by Natur

e and embroidered by imagination."

—Voltaire

The sublime color and scent of lavender is one of the many wonders of Provence.

The Temple, a former fishing lodge and garden folly that was once owned by the renowned David Hicks, is like a ray of eternal sunshine in the Dedham Vale of Suffolk, England, which is only sixty miles northeast of London. "It sits in the landscape like the Palladian ideal," says owner Veere Grenney, an interior designer who shares the residence with David Oliver, the design director of the Paint & Paper Library. "It's the best of both worlds: a palace and a cottage at the same time." They chose a pale palette for the interiors, a subtle and serene combination that supplements their landscape. Surrounded by green hedgerows and a reflecting pond with the temperamental British sky as a backdrop, the house has an ebullient presence that delights its owners, who have created an elegant and understated escape from their busy urban lives.

Crisp white trim and garden benches highlight the architecture of the converted fishing lodge. The landscape of hedges, lawns and vegetable beds is complemented by terra-cotta pots planted to overflowing with colorful geraniums.

ABOVE Rio, a whippet-terrier mix whose coloring matches the monochromatic decor, stands at an original double-hung sash window overlooking the canal. The Queen Anne chair is upholstered in antique linen and the armchair in faille. OPPOSITE The grand salon is a nuanced symphony of pale pinks and taupes. "I think because the main room is very formal, you need to downplay it with the furniture and fabric choices," says Grenney. "There's an eclectic mix of 18th- and 19th-century antiques along with other pieces that I designed and upholstered in my own fabrics, because it's more about comfort than anything else."

ABOVE The breakfast room is painted a pale, putty gray, which makes the space feel cool and tranquil. Furniture and flowers pop in such a subtle setting. OPPOSITE An antique Swedish bed was given a fresh coat of paint in the cozy, gray bedroom. The antique demilune table is also Swedish.

"Be daring, be differ[ent]

anything that will asse[rt]

and imaginative visi[on]

safers, the creatures of

slaves of the ordinary."

ent, be impractical, be

rt integrity of purpose

on against the play-it-

the commonplace, the

— *Cecil Beaton*

It's their mutual love of gardens and flowers that give the English and Italians an unerring color sense. They have a knack for creating rooms that don't necessarily have a color scheme per se, but nonetheless have a cohesive look based on well-chosen fabrics, art and antiques. The home formerly shared by Ashley and Allegra Hicks is a synthesis of their respective talents and pedigrees. He is an architect who was bred to be a decorator by his legendary father, David Hicks. She is the daughter of an Italian industrialist who studied design in Milan and trompe l'oeil in Brussels before moving to London where she worked as a decorative painter and designer of fabrics, carpets and furniture. Their combined aesthetic sense is in full bloom at their 19th-century house in London's Chelsea.

In the master bedroom, Ashley designed the theatrical bed hangings, which use the same printed cotton fabric as the head- and footboard. Allegra's chairs incorporate an image of themselves.

David Hicks was known for his bold use of color, especially red, and his son shares his Midas touch. In the drawing room, the 18th-century French chairs and sofa are covered in cottons the couple purchased on their frequent trips to India. Allegra designed the bindi kilim, red velvet flame chair and sawtoothed ottoman upholstered in traditional Fez embroidery. The cotton curtains have an appliquéd silk border. The room feels lively and melodic.

"Color is my daylong obs

ession, joy and torment."

—*Claude Monet*

At Giverny, the Impressionist painter Claude Monet's vine-covered house and gardens in the French countryside, red and pink tulips are brilliantly underplanted with blue forget-me-nots.

ABOVE Monet's gardens were a constant source of inspiration, a daily seminar in color theory, which allowed him to discover hidden depths of various hues in the flowers he so carefully planted. OPPOSITE There is nothing comparable to visiting Giverny and seeing Monet's beloved water lilies; it is like stepping into one of his paintings.

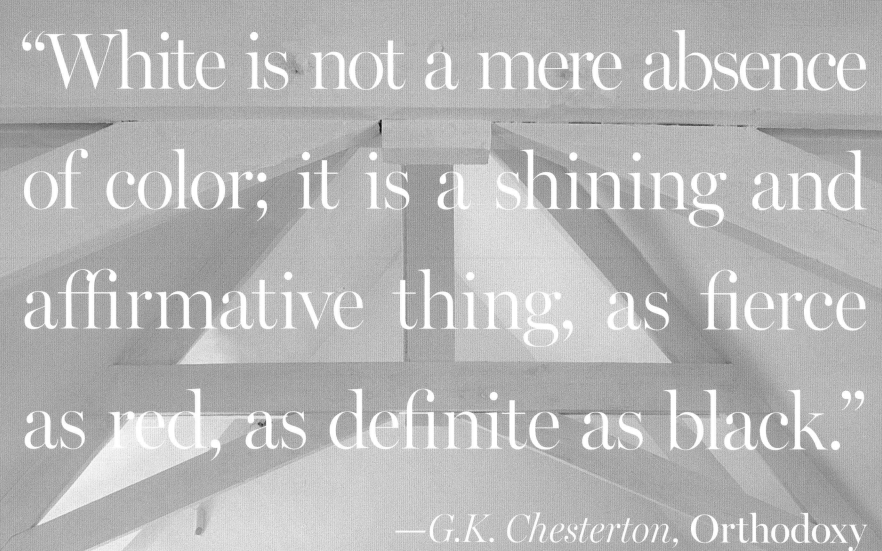

"White is not a mere absence of color; it is a shining and affirmative thing, as fierce as red, as definite as black."

—*G.K. Chesterton*, Orthodoxy

ABOVE A French 19th-century rocking chair of iron and linen in the all-white sitting room of Dick Vervoordt's farmhouse outside Antwerp. OPPOSITE With a fireplace and simple upholstered chairs, the all-white room is the ultimate place to escape reality, a color-free zone for contemplation, meditation and dreaming.

A SENSE

OF PLACE

The seat of the soul

A respect for preserving history and tradition is a foundation of European design. Continental and English decorating always incorporate references to the past. Honoring architecture and the landscape never goes out of style.

Althorp has been home to the Spencer family since 1508, and nineteen generations have left their mark on this storied estate in Northamptonshire. Its current steward is Charles Spencer, the brother of the late Princess Diana, who took over the reins of the house in 1992 when he was twenty-seven years old.

Inspired by his grandfather's knowledge of history and art, Charles came to know Althorp room by room, appreciating the collections of furniture and art—from English chairs commissioned by the 1st Earl Spencer in the 1750s to flamboyant French tables with ormolu tops. He made it his mission to make his ancestral home more relevant for the 21st century. He redecorated the rooms and rehung its collection of 650 paintings, preserving history while bringing it back to life.

Animals grazing on the lawns are essential to traditional English country life. "From the age of three or four," Earl Spencer remembers, "it was subtly impressed on me that, in time, I would be looking after one of England's great privately owned country houses."

ABOVE The marble-floored Woolton Hall is named after 18th-century equestrian painter John Woolton, whose oils encircle the room, as do Earl Spencer's favorite Hall chairs. The George I console is circa 1729 and the chandelier is circa 1759. OPPOSITE A 1745 painting of the Honorable John Spencer and son John, the 1st Earl Spencer, hangs over the mantel surrounded by other family portraits. In the corridor, a 1994 painting by Nelson Shanks of the 9th Earl's older sister, Diana, Princess of Wales.

Gustavian style is deeply rooted in the landscape and royal history of Sweden.

While the look—a mix of painted furniture with simple lines, gilded pieces, blue-and-white fabrics and porcelains, and sparkling crystal chandeliers—has been adapted by designers around the world, it is never more beguiling than in a true Scandinavian setting. Lars Sjöberg brings a missionary zeal to his restoration and decoration of traditional Swedish manor houses, preserving the glories of bygone days. At Säbylund, an 18th-century manor house in the countryside outside of Stockholm, he deftly and dramatically pays homage to Sweden's design heritage, an enriching combination of artistry, refinement, craftsmanship, practicality and restraint.

"The house has actually been lived in by the same family for 200 years," says Lars Sjöberg, a former curator at the National Museum in Stockholm, who used ruby red silk damask for the stool, bed, chairs, canopy and walls in a guest room.

The grand salon has sheer swags and jabots that feel opulent but not oppressive, letting in the precious light. Period mirrors and Pehr Ljung gilt-wood consoles offer elegant authenticity. The Swedish chairs are covered appropriately in damask and linen.

BELOW A collection of Swedish and French books line the library shelves where a medallion of the house's first owner still presides. The cane-backed chairs are English and the reading table is most likely Dutch or German. OPPOSITE The dining room is the epitome of refined Swedish style with a suite of Gustavian white-painted chairs and a canapé covered in Chinese silk damask, Bohemian wallpaper, family portraits and simply elegant sheer curtains.

Axel and May Vervoordt searched for a long time before finding the ideal site to build a vacation home in Verbier, Switzerland. But unlike other jet-set residents of the resort town, they wanted a simple, rustic retreat. Their chalet is the highest one in Verbier—1,300 feet above the town—and they have panoramic sunrise and sunset views.

To respect the landscape, the chalet was designed in the local vernacular both inside and out. They built their house with an underground garage so cars are never seen. "Everything in the house is very real—very simple. Nothing is done for the aesthetic. It is all done for the spirit," Axel says. "The silence of the snow and its spirit—is manifested in the majesty of the sky."

The furnishings, both old and new, are what Axel calls "Montagnard," which means they were hand-crafted by mountain dwellers, who have a great sense of minimalism and respect for wood, which enables them to make pieces that last for generations.

In the entrance hall—what Americans might call the mudroom—felt boots and 19th-century wicker baskets are lined up beneath a rustic 18th-century bench. In the Vervoordt household, May is responsible for the ambience—burning candles, delicious meals and wonderful flowers. In fact, she taught herself flower arranging by studying old Flemish still lifes.

In the sitting room, the fireplace mantel was made of three massive stone blocks. Axel designed the large, deep sofa. Behind it, a 16th-century Khmer terra-cotta vase was turned into a lamp. An 18th-century tabletop is hung like an artwork over the fireplace. The reclaimed wood throughout contributes to the house's appropriateness and sense of place.

ABOVE A view from the entrance hall to the living room, where French armchairs have cushions made of a vintage linen check. OPPOSITE In a guest room, the beds are built into an alcove. The red-and-white linens have a Swiss flair. The 19th-century rustic French armchair is made of beech and is the perfect seat for the soul.

Olive groves surround the 16th-century Tuscan farmhouse belonging to Mita Corsini Bland, a watercolorist who specializes in interiors, and Gerald Bland, a Madison Avenue decorative- and fine-arts dealer, who divide their time between New York City and Italy. Although they are connoisseurs, the couple wanted furnishings appropriate to the rural setting. "We knew we wanted some antique pieces, but only one or two per room," says Gerald. "And they needed to be good old-fashioned farmhouse furniture—nothing pretentious." Informed by the land and its history, they created a home that allows them to forget their demanding New York schedules and live in sync with the timeless rhythms of Italian country life.

Surrounded by a valley of olive trees that give the Blands' house its name—L'Uliveto—the historic farm still produces its own olive oil. Many of the trees are nearly 700 years old and living souls with a unique spirit of their own.

The mix of rustic furniture and contemporary art gives the living room its relaxed refinement. In the warmer months, the raised fireplace is used as a bar for the couple's frequent parties.

"I grew up
in a Villa—but
my dream was
always to live
in one of
the farmhouses
on the property.
A tremendous
gift from
my father."

—*Mita Bland*

The centerpiece of the dining room is a Tuscan table made of worm-eaten walnut surrounded by early 19th-century Italian chairs.

ABOVE The property's ancient cisterns and basins were repurposed as an outdoor entertaining space, where as many as two dozen people can dine under a pergola shaded by wisteria that blooms in March and again in June. OPPOSITE Nestled in a valley, the house embraces its bucolic site.

Old houses have an integrity and soul that in the right hands are never violated. A couple of French intellectuals are careful, respectful stewards of this 18th-century farmhouse in the far-flung Gers province of southwestern France, the heart of foie gras and Armagnac country. They have modernized it minimally, committed to maintaining its essential character and ambience. Basically undecorated, the house is furnished as a backdrop for family life and entertaining friends with meals prepared with produce from the local market. With heart-stopping views of the Pyrenees fifty miles to the south, the house embraces its surroundings, its perfect sense of place—the seat of the soul.

An espaliered fruit tree clings to the stone walls of the house. A pot of hydrangeas from the garden grace a weathered wood table where the owners often have lunch under the shade of ancient oak trees.

BELOW The entrance hall with its tall windows doubles as a dining room. A thirteen-foot-long late-Renaissance table stands on an Aubusson rug surrounded by simple, folding garden chairs. OPPOSITE The bones of the house—beams with a soulful patina and Medieval flagstone floors from an earlier 15th-century structure—imbue the kitchen with a rustic, timeless style. The massive stone fireplace is used for cooking, the cherrywood farm table for prep work and informal meals that celebrates their joie de vivre.

"They eat while the corks fly and there is talk, laughter and merriment."

—*Jean Brillat-Savarin*

Seek inspiration and harm

ny from nature.

In the heart of the Swedish province of Västergötland, where monasteries and noble estates have stood proudly since the Middle Ages, Lars Sjöberg found remnants of a great estate known as Salaholm that he felt compelled to rescue. The horizontal timber structure dates to 1802, and his renovation and decoration are a scrupulous homage to the property's past. Surrounded by a dark pine forest that was once field and meadows crisscrossed by stone walls, the house is a time capsule. The furnishings, both antiques and impeccable reproductions, hew to the principles of 18th-century Swedish design that followed patterns developed in Holland, England and France during the Baroque period.

Lars Sjöberg preserved the patina of Salahom and the Popsicle-stick boards that give the house a touch of whimsy and charm. It is the quintessence of Swedish country style: spare and informal, rustic and refined.

"The renovation was initiated with a sense of urgent purpose, to restore an air of freshness."

—*Lars Sjöberg*

PREVIOUS PAGE The kitchen shelves display a collection of Chinese export porcelain developed during the Swedish East India Company's heyday from the 1730s to the early 19th century. BELOW Lars Sjöberg's magic touch is evident in the way he infuses his house with the spirit of past lives, decorating rooms the way they might or should have been.

ABOVE Tall clocks were an important element in 18th-century Swedish homes. This gray-painted rococo clock has a dial dated 1763. CENTER King Gustav III favored the sheaf motif on his 18th-century chairs because it evoked the coat of arms of an earlier Swedish king and ancestor, Gustav Vasa.

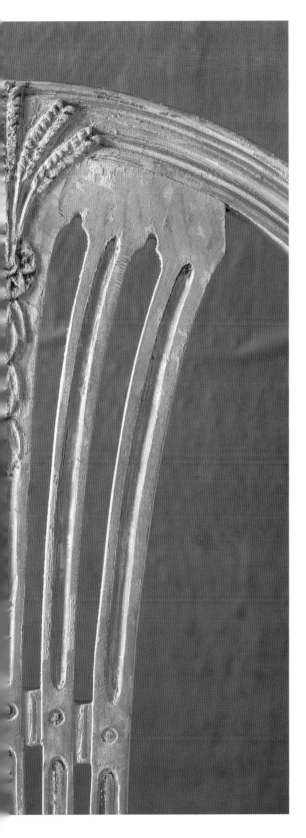

ABOVE Sjöberg—who has trained carpenters to adopt historical techniques to hand-craft furniture according to 18th-century designs—displays their work in an idealized context.

"At a time when the count

and fields and pastures

aquiring a decaying estate

with peeling paint and an

a stimulating prospect."

ryside is being abandoned,

give way to deforestation,

is a challenge. A mansion

overgrown garden can be

– Lars Sjöberg

In the country, houses are wedded to the landscape. The romance of rural life is a marriage of architecture and horticulture. When Parisian antiques dealer Sylvain Lévy-Alban found a property in the Loire Valley with a crumbling medieval abbey surrounded by ten acres of ancient stone walls, orchards and clusters of mature beeches, chestnuts and magnolias, he was immediately smitten.

"I fell in love with the spirit of the place, the mystery, the big walls, the ruins," he says. "I thought the property was wonderful." With his unerring eye, he resurrected the gardens, creating multifaceted, enchanting, verdant spaces. Le Prieuré de Notre Dames des Marchais is a vision of paradise to be cherished and enjoyed.

For a gardener, the mudroom/potting room is the most important space in the house, and Sylvain Lévy-Alban furnished his with sturdy antiques set against walls adorned with 17th- and 18th-century blue-and-white Portuguese tiles.

ABOVE An 18th-century terra-cotta statue of Bacchus presides over one of the many gardens on the ten-acre property in the Loire Valley. OPPOSITE The ruins of a 12th-century abbey give structure to the rose garden with its plantings of lavender, yews, topiary and Dorothy Perkins roses.

In the herb garden, artichokes, fennel, thyme and dill are as decorative as they are delicious.

The British-born, California-based interior decorator Kathryn M. Ireland is a whirlwind. She designed her countryside retreat in south-western France as a sanctuary where friends, family and food are paramount. Once a working farm and vineyard, the rambling property fulfilled a childhood dream.

"Everyone loves to come here," says Ireland, who is famous for her spontaneous and creative *Art de Vivre*. "It's not chichi at all." The style of the house is an artful articulation of her wide-ranging sensibility. "The architecture feels a bit Tuscan, the landscape reminds me of England, and the rest is French. It brought together all of the places that symbolize relaxation to me.... Life slows down here....," says Ireland.

Chickens roam freely through the doorway that has curtains made from Kathryn Ireland's own playful and colorful printed fabric. The simplicity of the foyer reflects the laid-back spirit of the house that is meant for decompression and recreation.

The sunny, beamed kitchen is a former cow barn, which is kept warm by an Aga stove. Loom Italia wicker chairs in vibrant red surround a 19th-century English pine table. "Cooking and eating is a way of life here," says Ireland. "I have a knack for finding fabulous people who might not necessarily encounter each other and bringing them together."

ABOVE "The days are very long," says Ireland of her old-fashioned French summers. "It doesn't get dark until 10:30. You get to do the things that everyone used to do." OPPOSITE Indoors or outdoors, every meal is treated like a celebration at the house just north of Toulouse. "I prepare dishes from whatever shows up in the garden," she says, "endless Niçoise salads, gazpacho, great quiches, onion tarts, pizzas."

To grow a beautiful future

s to honor the past....

Fields of sunflowers surround Kathyrn Ireland's classic Quercy farmhouse in an under-the-radar region just north of Toulouse.

When the iconic 20th-century architect Mies van der Rohe famously said, "Less is more," he probably wasn't thinking about an 18th-century Swedish manor house. Nevertheless, Lars Sjöberg has applied this philosophy to the twenty-five-room manor house called Regnaholm, where his family has gathered to celebrate holidays for generations.

Decorated elegantly in period style, the house has a spare modernity that has served as inspiration for the designers of IKEA who have made pilgrimages to study and absorb its gestalt. "Our goals at Regnaholm have always been the restoration of such authentic beauty," says Sjöberg, "and of an authentic simple life."

Framed by freshly fallen snow, the yellow stone manor house seems especially majestic and welcoming. Because of its size, the house is difficult to heat, and the family relies on tiled stoves with their clever smoke-circulation system, invented in 1767, to stay warm. FOLLOWING PAGE The extra-long sofa and high tea table are icons of Swedish design. Most of the furnishings in the house are exacting reproductions made by Sjöberg's father, Bengt, who was a cabinetmaker and teacher.

"This was not to be a museum. It's a gathering place for our family."

—Lars Sjöberg

"Even in the brief hours of daylight we burn candles at the table—in the candlesticks, sconces and chandeliers," says Sjöberg, whose father made the reproduction chairs and wall sconces in the dining room. The bust of Swedish King Charles XII is mid 18th-century.

BELOW The sunny kitchen has walls painted yellow and white, which are the ideal backdrop for displaying blue-and-white china. Two demi-lune tables pushed together make it possible for the entire family to have breakfast together. OPPOSITE A bedroom has a Shaker austerity and peacefulness with every object and piece of furniture treated with utmost respect.

May and Axel Vervoordt's fifty-room castle outside of Antwerp is one of the most welcoming homes in Europe. Twice a year, the couple opens the doors to design connoisseurs who come not only to admire, and be inspired by, their beautifully decorated rooms but also to shop because the castle doubles as the showroom for Axel's antiques business, which caters to diverse sensibilities.

"I adore mixing things, bringing objects together in the way that you would people," he says. "They enrich one another, sometimes because they are in harmony, sometimes because they are opposed in spirit and play off one another." Nobody has as much personal style as Axel, who instinctively knows that the magic is in the mix.

Axel Vervoordt's home is his castle. Built during the Middle Ages, the castle of 's-Gravenwezel stands in a Flemish landscape that recalls some vestiges of its 18th-century plans.

A library with a cabinet of curiosities is one of many rooms at the Vervoordts' estate that speaks to many vernaculars. Nature, art and philosophy have had a large impact on his life and work, as he says. The room is filled with treasures he has collected. Like everything he does, the room is unpretentious, yet sophisticated.

The castle has fifty rooms, and the Vervoordts wanted them to have distinct personalities. Their upstairs sitting room is the Oriental salon. A 1972 painting by Antoni Tàpies dominates the space. The asteroid-like bronze sculpture is by Lucio Fontana. The sofa and club chairs are from the Axel Vervoordt Kanaal home collection, which defines their personal style.

The kitchen is as functional as it is elegant with a white Aga stove and a bold brass chandelier. The cupboards are painted pale blue to showcase the Vervoordts' extensive collection of china. An unfinished, hand-hewn wood table is a welcoming spot for informal meals.

DE WIJDE WERELD

ABOVE The magnificently landscaped grounds were designed by Vervoordt's frequent collaborator Jacques Wirtz, who worked from architect Jan Pieter van Baurscheit's original 18th-century plans. The horse and rider feel at home in the garden.

es and dreams—is the fabric of life.

CENTER An arbor provides a shaded outdoor space for dining, and cool retreat for the Vervoordts' dog. RIGHT An antique bench frames a view of the gardens, which are treated as outdoor rooms that establish an unmistakable sense of place.

ACKNOWLEDGMENTS

The world of interiors takes on a different light, depending on how you look at it. Exceptional photographers are responsible for capturing these images that reveal the essence of a place. With that in mind, this book is dedicated in memory of my dear friend Jacques Dirand, one of the most talented and well-known French photographers, whom I had the great pleasure of working with for nearly 20 years before his death in 2009. His artistic technique and creative use of light, lenses and perspective are unparalleled. He shot most of the stories in this book and produced memorable photographs for a wealth of international magazines such as Maision & Jardin, Decoration Internationale, Elle Decoration, Vogue Deco, The World of Interiors and, of course, Veranda. To this day when I am producing a shoot I know he is with me—and I say merci, Jacques, for all that you taught me. We miss you, xo, Carolyn

There are many wonderful and special people whom I want to sincerely thank for their support and contribution to *Veranda* and to this book. My heartfelt thanks to:

All the incredible homeowners, designers, architects and antique dealers who have opened their homes and shared their projects with *Veranda* and me. For this book in particular, a special thanks to: Andrew Allfree, Roberto Bergero, Gerald and Mita Bland, Isabelle de Borchgrave, Pierro Castellini, Bruno de Caumont, Jean-Loup Daraux, Jean-Philippe Demeyer, the Fabrizio family, Alain and Brigitte Garnier, Giverny Foundation, Jacques Grange, Giles Gregoire, Veere Grenney and David Oliver, Susan Gutfreund, Michelle and Yves Halard, Allegra Hicks, Ashley Hicks, David Hicks, Kathryn Ireland, Michel Klein and Joel Fournier, Christian Liaigre, Sylvain Lévy-Alban and Charlie Garnett, Frédéric Méchiche, Henri Samuel, Steven Shubel, Lars Sjöberg, Charles Spada, Earl Charles Spencer, Axel and May Vervoordt, and Dick Vervoordt.

Each of the wonderfully talented photographers whose beautiful photographs have made this book possible. A sincere thanks to each of you: Alexandre Bailhache, Jacques Dirand, Miguel Flores-Vianna, Oberto Gili, Thibault Jeanson, Staffan Johansson, Massimo Listri, Rene Stoeltie, Simon Upton, Mikkel Vang, Fritz von der Schulenburg, Elizabeth Zeschin.

The Hearst Corporation who acquired *Veranda* in 2002; and Jacqueline Deval, publisher of Hearst Books, for believing in this book and for her knowledge, guidance, patience and support.

The Sterling Publishing team: Chris Thompson, art director, for his genuine enthusiasm, generosity of spirit and keen eye for color and graphics, thank you for helping to interpret my vision. Alexandra Brodsky, Sal Destro, Mary Hern and Elana Mitchel, for your attention to detail, consistent follow through and for keeping us on schedule.

Susan Uedelhofen, the designer who artfully actualized my vision for the book. And Rich Michels, for his dedication to *Veranda* as art director.

Kathryn Marx, who tirelessly and willingly gathered photography from the archives, and helped to facilitate the editing process of the images being consider.

Mario Lopez-Cordero, Meeghan Truelove and Dan Shaw—for the very special part that you contributed each step of the way that without a doubt made all the difference.

Marina Weisburg and Dayle Wood—who worked in the very early stages to pull and catalogue all the tear sheets for the stories I wanted to include in this book.

Dominique Tailleux—it's the "dealers eye" that brings the wonderfully special antiques and objets des curiosities to light, for us to see, contemplate and ultimately collect and cherish.

The wonderful and talented editors I've had the privilege to work with throughout my career, with an extra special thanks to Dara Caponigro and Lisa Newsom, who supported me in doing this book, and Margaret Kennedy and Lou Gropp, who encouraged and helped make it possible for me to go to Paris.

Clint Smith, for writing the Preface and your leadership as editor in chief at *Veranda*.

Charlotte Moss, one of the most knowledgeable, talented, inspiring and articulate women that I know and respect— thank you for writing the Foreword.

All the dedicated staff members, past and present, and contributing editors, writers and producers, thank you for your talented contributions, perseverance and consummate professionalism.

CREDITS

Photo

Front cover: Simon Upton
Back cover: Alexandre Bailhache
Author photo: Max Kim-Bee

Alexandre Bailhache: 2, 15 (bottom right), 25-29, 72-75, 97-101, 225-231, 251-255, 288

Jacques Dirand: 7 (top right), 13, 15 (top left), 37-43, 53-59, 67-71, 91-95, 103-109, 112-115, 117-121, 130-135, 137-141, 155-159, 161-165, 173-179, 195-201, 202-203, 217-223, 273-281, 283

Miguel Flores-Vianna: 7 (bottom right), 15 (bottom left), 19-23, 46-51, 211-215

Oberto Gili: 181-185

Thibault Jeanson: 7 (top left), 9, 61-65, 77-81, 123-129

Staffan Johansson: 15 (top right), 150-153, 241-247, 265-271

Massimo Listri: 31-35
Fritz von der Schulenburg: 5, 207-209

Simon Upton: 7 (bottom left), 11, 85-89, 145-149, 187-191

Mikkel Vang: 257-263

Elizabeth Zeschin: 233-239

All stories produced by Carolyn Englefield, with the exception of:

Miguel Flores-Vianna: 18-23; 46-51; 144-149; 152-153; 211-215; 240-249

David Oliver: 186-191

Deborah Sanders and Miguel Flores-Vianna: 206-208

INDEX